WAYNE ROONEY

RORY CALLAN

Wayne Rooney is one
of the most talented
footballers in the world.
Read all about his
club and international
football career inside –
then flip over to find
out more about
Jermain Defoe.

D1628012

B000 000 013 3403

ABERDEEN LIBRARIES

This edition 2014

Franklin Watts
338 Euston Road
London NW1 3BH

Franklin Watts Australia
Level 17/207 Kent Street
Sydney NSW 2000

Text © Rory Callan 2012
Design © Franklin Watts 2012

Series editor: Adrian Cole
Art director: Jonathan Hair
Design: Steve Prosser
Picture research: Diana Morris

The author has asserted his rights
in accordance with the Copyright,
Designs and Patents Act, 1988.

All rights reserved

A CIP catalogue record of this book
is available from the British Library

pb ISBN: 978 1 4451 0213 9
Library ebook ISBN: 978 1 4451 3735 3

Dewey classification: 796.3'34'092

Printed in China

Franklin Watts is a division of
Hachette Children's Books,
an Hachette UK company.
www.hachette.co.uk

796.3340922

Wayne Rooney
Contents

ENGLAND'S BOY WONDER

2004 European Championships
England vs Switzerland, Portugal

It's a blazing 37°C in the Portuguese city of Coimbra. England are about to face Switzerland in their second game of the European Championships. The stadium is full – England must win this game if they are to qualify for the **quarter-finals** of the tournament. All eyes are on Wayne Rooney, an 18-year-old striker from Liverpool. The newspapers have called him "Boy Wonder".

23 minutes

England start well; their passing is good and Rooney is using his skill and power to cause the Switzerland defenders problems. After 23 minutes, Michael Owen crosses the ball into the **penalty box**. Rooney jumps and headers the ball, powering it past the goalkeeper. GOAL! Rooney runs towards the England fans to celebrate, doing a back flip on the way! The goal puts Rooney in the record books as the youngest player to have scored in the European Championships.

75 minutes

To round off an outstanding performance, Rooney scores another goal in the second half with a powerful shot from outside the box. Rooney sets up England for a well-deserved 3–0 victory.

England vs Croatia, Stadio de Luz, Lisbon

Four days later, Rooney scores another two goals – this time against Croatia. His first goal is spectacular; a blistering shot from 30 metres out sends the ball travelling into the net at 80 kph. For an 18-year-old, his power, skill and scoring ability are incredible. His 5-star performance earns him the "Man of the Match Award" and guarantees England's place in the quarter-finals.

▲ *Rooney celebrates scoring the opening goal in the match against Switzerland in 2004.*

Number one

In the space of a week, Rooney introduced himself to fans around the world as football's new superstar. Just three years before, he was sitting in school preparing for his GCSE exams – now he was England's number-one striker. ***But how did he get there?***

EARLY DAYS

Wayne Rooney was born on the 24 October, 1985, in Liverpool. He grew up on the Croxteth housing estate on the north side of Liverpool City. He lived in an ordinary **council house** with his mum, dad and two younger brothers, Graeme and John. His dad had always been a devoted Everton supporter. He went to every Everton match he could get a ticket for and brought Wayne to his first Everton match when he was only 6 months old!

Everton Academy

Wayne's football talent was first noticed when he was playing with his local team in an Under-10s match. The Everton **scouts** at the game were very impressed by his skill, bravery and goal-scoring ability. As a result, they invited him to start training at the Everton Academy. As soon as he joined, the Everton **coaches** knew that they had someone special on their hands. Rooney's flair for goal scoring was obvious to everyone who saw him play. One of his Under-11 coaches wrote in his end of year report that:

"Wayne is the best natural goal scorer I've seen."

In one season, Rooney's Under-11 team played 30 games against other clubs from all over England. He scored in every match, netting 114 goals in total. In one of the games he scored nine goals!

▶ *Rooney during an England Under-15s match against Spain.*

MAKING THE BREAKTHROUGH

Rooney made his Everton first team **debut** in August 2002 against Tottenham Hotspur at Goodison Park. He was 16 years old. However, it was his first Premiership goal against Arsenal at Goodison Park that made the whole football world sit up and take notice.

First Premiership goal

Arsenal were on an incredible unbeaten run of 30 games and were expected to steamroll over Everton. With the game at 1–1, Rooney came on as a **substitute** in the second half. He received the ball inside the Everton half and took a few steps forward. He looked around, but there was no Everton player near him to take a pass. Instead, he blasted the ball from 30 yards out towards the Arsenal goal. The ball came off the underside of the crossbar and crashed into the net, leaving Arsenal goalkeeper David Seaman with no chance of saving it.

A very special player

The goal was replayed on TV for days after and the whole country became aware of the name Wayne Rooney. The Arsenal manager, Arsene Wenger, said after the game that:

"...Rooney is the biggest English talent I've seen since I arrived in England. We were beaten by a special goal from a very special player."

▲ *Rooney in his Everton first-team tracksuit. Playing for Everton in the Premier League was a dream come true for Rooney.*

Wayne and Manchester United

After playing for England in the European Championship Finals in 2004, Rooney wanted to play in the Champions League against the best players in Europe. The Manchester United manager Sir Alex Ferguson was determined to **sign** him, and he offered Everton a massive £27 million. This made Rooney the most expensive teenage footballer in the world. Sir Alex Ferguson said:

"...we have got the best young player this country has seen in the past 30 years."

At Old Trafford

After Rooney had spent his first week at Manchester United, he knew he had made the right choice. Everything about the club was bigger and better; the training pitches, the coaches, the players and, of course, the manager. Even the subs' bench at Old Trafford had heated seats so the players didn't freeze when watching the game on a cold winter Saturday afternoon!

Hat-trick hero

Rooney made a dream debut for Manchester United in a **UEFA** Champions League match against Turkish League champions, Fenerbache. Old Trafford was packed with fans eager to see their new star signing. Wayne didn't disappoint them. He scored a **hat trick**, with two goals in the first half and a stunning free kick in the second half. United fans were delighted and Rooney was already on his way to becoming an idol at Old Trafford.

▲ *Rooney poses for the press cameras shortly after signing for Manchester United. At the time, he was the most expensive 18-year-old footballer in the world.*

THAT WINNING FEELING

For Rooney the 2007/08 season was the most successful of his career so far. His 18 goals and his creative play made him a vital part of the team. Manchester United had already won the Premier League, could they "do the double" by winning the Champions League too?

Champions League Final, 2008

In 2008, for the first time in its history, the Champions League Final was between two English clubs – Manchester United and Chelsea. It was Rooney's first Champions League Final. He said before the game that:

"...playing in the final is a great opportunity to show the world what I can do."

The first half

The Final was held in Moscow's Luzhniki Stadium. The first half was controlled by Manchester United, and they took the lead after 26 minutes when Cristiano Ronaldo scored from a header. They kept control of the game for most of the first half, but Chelsea's Frank Lampard scored an **equaliser** two minutes before half time.

The second half

The second half was tense and tough. Chelsea controlled much of the play, and nearly scored for a second time. When the whistle blew after 90 minutes, the game went to extra time. Rooney had played really well on the night, but just didn't get any clear cut goal-scoring chances.

Penalty shootout

No goals were scored in extra time, and everyone in the stadium waited nervously for the penalty shootout. Manchester United won the shootout 6–5, earning Rooney the most valuable medal in club football, and Manchester United the double.

▼ Rooney lifts the Champions League trophy after Manchester United won a thrilling penalty shootout against Chelsea in 2008.

SIMPLY STUNNING

In 2012, Rooney won the 20 Seasons Award "Premier League Goal" category for his overhead kick against Manchester City. The goal was one of the most spectacular ever seen at Old Trafford. A cross from team-mate Nani was going high and behind Rooney, who was waiting in the penalty box. Rooney acted instinctively; he adjusted his position and sprung into the air, belting the ball past Joe Hart in the City goal with a fierce overhead kick. It was a stunning finish. To make the goal even more perfect, it gave United a 2–1 victory over their city rivals!

Fifth Premier League medal

In April 2013, Rooney helped Manchester United defeat Aston Villa 3–0 at Old Trafford. This victory earned United their 20th English League title, putting them two titles ahead of Liverpool. For Rooney it was a fifth Premier League medal.

Sir Alex retires

Two weeks after winning the League, Manchester United's manager, Sir Alex Ferguson, announced his retirement. He had spent 27 years at the club, becoming the most successful manager in the history of British football. Rooney had become a star at Old Trafford under Sir Alex's coaching guidance and skill.

An all-time great

Rooney continued to score goals for United. He is the club's fourth-highest goal scorer of all time, with over 200 first-team goals. By the time Rooney retires there is a chance he will have broken Sir Bobby Charlton's record of 249 goals for Manchester United.

If he achieves this target he will go down as one of the all-time greats at Old Trafford.

When David Moyes became manager of Manchester United in July 2013, people thought Rooney might transfer to another club. However, in February 2014, he signed a new five-year contract with United – worth £300,000 a week – making Rooney one of the highest-paid sports stars in the world.

▼ Rooney in action for Manchester United against Olympiacos in 2014.

LIVING THE DREAM – PLAYING FOR ENGLAND

Rooney was the most talented youth player in England, with an incredible goal-scoring record. He started his international career when he was picked to play with the Under-15 and Under-17 England teams. Rooney didn't get the chance to progress to the Under-19 and the Under-21 teams. At the age of 17, his ability was so good he was chosen to play for the full England team.

◀ Rooney takes the ball forward in his England full-team debut against Australia on 12 February, 2003. England lost the match 1–3.

Starting with the full England team

In February 2003, Rooney was called by Sven-Goran Eriksson to train with the full England squad before a friendly match against Australia. Rooney entered the record books when he came on as a substitute in the second half. At 17 years and 111 days, he became the youngest player to ever play for England. From then on he played in all the qualifying games for Euro 2004. His first goal for his country came against Macedonia in September 2003. After Theo Walcott, he is the second youngest player to have scored for England.

WORLD CUP 2006 DREAMS

When he was a kid Wayne used to wear an England **replica** jersey around his estate, and pretend to be playing for his country. Never in his wildest dreams did he think that he would get all the way to the World Cup – for real!

Disaster strikes!

Rooney's preparations for the World Cup were going well when disaster struck. In one of the last games of the 2005/2006 season against Chelsea, he went down after a heavy challenge. The crowd went silent as they saw him stretchered off the pitch. The injury turned out to be quite serious – a broken bone in his foot, called the metatarsal. This broken bone would stop him playing football for at least six weeks. The news was a serious blow to England's World Cup hopes. For Rooney, it felt as if all his dreams of playing in the World Cup were falling apart.

Rooney stays focused

Rooney decided to do everything he could to get himself fit in time for the World Cup. He did a lot of work in the gym to keep in shape. Instead of running, he went swimming and cycling every day to keep his fitness levels up. Just days before the tournament was due to start he was declared fit to play.

▲ *Rooney arrives at hospital to have a scan on his foot before the 2006 World Cup Finals.*

WORLD CUP 2006

England finished top of their group and then went on to defeat Ecuador 1–0 in the next round. Rooney played the full 90 minutes and could feel his match sharpness coming back to him. He couldn't wait to get stuck into Portugal in the quarter-finals.

England vs Portugal, World Cup quarter finals

The match atmosphere was very tense, and there were hardly any scoring chances in the first half. Then, early in the second half, Rooney received the ball, but he was fouled by three Portugal players. As he stumbled to the ground, he stamped on one of them – Ricardo Carvahlo. The referee gave Rooney a straight red card, and he was sent off.

After extra time the game ended 0–0, and went to a penalty shootout. England lost 4–1. If Rooney hadn't been sent off, England might have gone on to the World Cup semi final.

▲ *Rooney is shown a red card by the referee, and is sent off.*

WORLD CUP 2010

After scoring 34 goals for Manchester United during the 2009/2010 season and collecting the PFA Player of the Year Award, Rooney was ready for the 2010 World Cup in South Africa. Along with Messi, Ronaldo and Kaká, 24-year-old Rooney was expected to be one of the star players.

Twisted ankle

Then Rooney was hit by some bad luck. In a Champions League match against Bayern Munich, he twisted his ankle in the very last minute of the game. By the end of May the injury had cleared up and Rooney was back training with the England squad. But the injury seemed to have taken the sharpness out of his game.

England vs Slovenia, World Cup Finals, Group C

Rooney put in a good performance against Slovenia in the final Group C game. He looked full of energy, and was passing and controlling the ball well. Then, with 18 minutes remaining, his right ankle began to swell up, and he had to be substituted.

England vs Germany, World Cup Finals, knockout stage

Rooney recovered to play against Germany in the first knockout round. Unfortunately, Germany were in brilliant form and they crushed England 4–1.

EUROPEAN CHAMPIONSHIP 2012

Rooney missed the opening games of Euro 2012 against France and Sweden due to a two-match suspension. When he did make his first appearance against Ukraine, he scored the only goal of the match to put England through to the quarter finals.

England played Italy in an energy-sapping quarter final. It was not an easy game for Rooney. He had to do plenty of chasing and pressing as Italy kept possession. After a goalless 90 minutes and extra time, the game went to a penalty shootout. Even after two hours of play, Rooney still had enough energy to score one of England's penalties. Unfortunately England's bad luck in penalty shootouts continued. They lost 4–2 and were knocked out.

▲ *Rooney was exhausted after the match against Germany.*
On the day, Germany had just been too good for England.

Brazil 2014

In February 2013, Rooney captained England for the first time when they took on Brazil in a friendly game at Wembley Stadium. England beat the five-time World Champions 2–1, with Rooney scoring the first goal of the match.

In 2013, the England team travelled to Brazil to mark the reopening of the world-famous Maracanã Stadium, the venue for the 2014 World Cup final. Rooney scored England's second goal of the match, securing a 2–2 draw.

World Cup qualification

Rooney was England's top scorer in the World Cup qualifying group stages, with seven goals. Rooney said afterwards:

"It's been a good campaign, the aim was to finish top of the group and that's what we've done."

But it wasn't as easy as England would have liked. Instant qualification hinged on the final group game against Poland. Luckily Rooney was on top form and put England 1–0 up with a powerful header. The match finished 2–0 to England.

Rooney is now one of England's most capped players. When asked in an interview what he expects from the 2014 World Cup he said:

"I want to try to perform. It's my 10th or 11th year playing for England, so the obvious goal is to be successful and win trophies. That would be the icing on the cake. Hopefully, I can do that."

▼ Rooney wins a header during England's World Cup Group H qualifying match against San Marino.

TIMELINE GLOSSARY

Team	Appearances	Goals
League		
2002–04 Everton	67	15
2004– Manchester United	433	210
National		
2000–01 England U-15	4	2
2001–02 England U-17	12	7
2002 England U-19	1	0
2003–Sept 2011 England	85	38

Coaches People who train athletes, in this case footballers.

Council house House built and owned by the local council to rent out to local people.

Debut First appearance, in this case as a player in a particular team.

Equaliser Used to describe the goal that brings both teams to the same score.

Hat trick Three goals scored by one player in the same match.

Penalty box A marked rectangle on a football pitch, with the goal in the centre, inside which players take penalty shots.

Replica An exact copy.

Quarter-finals Eight teams compete in the quarter-finals to win a place in the semi-finals.

Scouts In this case, the people whose job it is to look out for talented players.

Sign [for] Sign a contract that commits the player to a particular team.

Subs/Substitutes Players who are ready to take over, should one of their team be injured or become tired.

UEFA Union of European Football Associations.

INDEX

TIMELINE GLOSSARY

Team	Appearances	Goals
League		
1999–2004 West Ham United	93	29
2000–2001 Bournemouth (loan)	29	18
2004–2008 Tottenham Hotspur	139	43
2008 Portsmouth (loan)	1	1
2008–2009 Portsmouth	30	14
2009–2014 Tottenham Hotspur	135	47
2014– Toronto FC		
National		
2001–2003 England U21	23	7
2004– England	46	15

Adrenalin A chemical (hormone) released by the body to increase the heart rate.

Caps The word used in sport to show that the player represented their national team.

Coaching Training given to athletes by coaches.

Council house House built and owned by the local council to rent out to local people.

Debut First appearance, in this case as a player in a particular team.

Dribble Travelling with the ball using a series of short kicks.

Elite Exceptionally good.

Hat-trick Three goals scored by one player in the same match.

Loan In football, a period of time spent by a footballer playing for a club that is not the club he or she is signed to, usually to gain experience.

Marker Player whose job it is to track, or "mark", a player on the opposite team.

Penalty box A marked rectangle on a football pitch, with the goal in the centre, inside which players take penalty shots.

Professional Professional football teams are made up of players for whom football is their paid job.

UEFA Union of European Football Associations.

INDEX

way by scoring a stunning hat trick. He was delighted after the match, telling reporters that the three goals were **"the sweetest hat trick of my career"**. He also created a bit of history by becoming the first player to score a hat trick in the new Wembley!

WORLD CUP 2014

Defoe played his part in helping England qualify for the 2014 World Cup in Brazil. He played in four of England's World Cup qualifying games, scoring three times. After signing for Toronto FC in January 2014, Defoe made it clear that he still wanted to be in the England squad for the 2014 World Cup.

"Hopefully I can be on the plane. I would like to think that the England manager – and everyone in England – knows what I can do, what I bring to the team. If selected I'll be ready."

▼ *Defoe controls the ball in the UEFA Euro 2012 Group G qualifying match against Bulgaria.*

England vs Slovenia, World Cup 2010

The highlight of Defoe's World Cup experience was against Slovenia in the final group game. In a must win game for England, he scored the only goal of the match with a neat volley from six yards out. The goal was enough for England to go through to the last 16. In an emotional interview after the game Defoe said:

"I'm lost for words, what a moment! As a young lad you dream of doing it one day. It's brilliant we've won."

EUROPEAN CHAMPIONSHIP 2012

England were eventually knocked out in the quarter-final stages by Germany, but Defoe continued his good form for England after the World Cup. In September 2010, he was once again the star as England thrashed Bulgaria 4–0 at Wembley Stadium. It was England's first qualification game for Euro 2012. Defoe led the

◄ *Defoe celebrates with his team-mates after scoring against Slovenia.*

When Defoe and his team-mates landed at Tambo Airport in Johannesburg, South Africa, thousands of South Africans were there to cheer on their heroes. The England team were one of the best supported at the World Cup, because many players were familiar from Premier League games shown on TV across Africa.

Due to the high altitude, Defoe found the first few days of training tough. The team was based in a five-star luxury hotel in the city of Rustenburg, situated at 1,500 metres above sea level. At this height there is less oxygen in the air, making it difficult to breathe. After seven days though, all the players had started to adjust.

▼ Defoe in action against Algeria at the World Cup Finals, 2010.

SOUTH AFRICA 2010

▲ *The official England team photo showing the South Africa 2010 squad. Defoe is top left.*

For months before the World Cup, Defoe had been looking forward to playing for his country in front of a world-wide audience. As he was growing up in Beckton, he watched all of England's World Cup games with his family on TV. After each game he went on to the street to try to copy the skills of his heroes. For the first time he wouldn't be watching the games, he'd be at the centre of the action.

World Cup 2006

Slowly, Defoe established himself as a regular on the England team. His performances in the qualifying games for the 2006 World Cup were very impressive. He scored vital goals in these games, and was looking forward to going to his first World Cup in Germany. When Sven-Goran Eriksson announced his 23-man squad for the tournament, everybody expected Defoe to be included. However, in a shock move, Eriksson decided to leave out Defoe, selecting Theo Walcott of Arsenal instead.

The English public and media were baffled by the decision. Naturally, Defoe was extremely disappointed to be left out. It was a hard knock to take after looking forward for so long to playing in the World Cup.

Defoe did his best to accept the decision calmly. He didn't become bitter and angry with the England management; that wasn't his style. Instead, he worked harder than ever at his game and made a vow that he would do everything in his power to make it back on to the team. By the time the next World Cup came around in 2010, Defoe was one of the stars on the England team.

◄ *Defoe cuts inside one of Austria's defenders during a 2006 World Cup qualifier.*

England Under-21s

Defoe went on to gain 23 **caps** for the Under-21s, scoring seven goals between 2001–2003. He enjoyed playing at Under-21 level, but by now he wanted to be on the England first team. His club form with West Ham United was excellent; he finished top scorer for the club two seasons in a row. Then, in 2004, he got a call from Sven-Goran Eriksson, the England manager. He invited Defoe to train with the England first team, before a friendly match with Sweden.

England first team

Defoe was so excited when he stepped onto the England training ground. Some of the best players in the world were there, including David Beckham, Wayne Rooney, John Terry and Steven Gerrard. They looked like such fierce rivals when they played against each other with their clubs, but here they were laughing and joking like best mates!

▲ *Defoe during an England first team training session in 2004.*

ENGLAND CALLING

From an early age it looked very likely that Defoe would become a professional footballer. But would he ever make it at international level? To be picked as one of the best 11 footballers in England means you have to be an exceptional player.

Defoe devoted himself to football. He practised endlessly, followed a training routine and improved his strength. He did everything to make the most of the talent he was born with.

England Under-15 and Under-18 levels

Defoe was just 14 years old when he went to spend two years at the FA's National Sports Centre. Soon after, Defoe was picked to play for England Under-15s, and then the Under-18s. These international games gave him valuable experience. He got used to travelling and began to learn about playing against other nations.

▼ *Defoe heads the ball during an England Under-21 match against Greece in 2001.*

The Wigan defence began to crack, and within seven minutes Defoe scored another two goals. Most players would take it easy after scoring a **hat trick**, but Defoe wasn't finished. He continued to push forward. He was out-playing the Wigan players, and rifled in another two goals to take his total to five. When the final whistle blew, the match ended 9–1, and Defoe entered the history books as only the third man to score five goals in a league match.

UEFA Champions League

Performances like this from Defoe helped Tottenham to reach the quarter finals of the Champions League in 2011. Playing in Europe really suited Defoe's style of play. In October 2013 he scored his 23rd goal in European football, making him Tottenham's all-time highest scorer in European matches.

Toronto FC

In January 2014, after signing for the Canadian side Toronto FC, Defoe went to play Major League Soccer (MLS). He travels all over North America to play teams such as LA Galaxy, D.C. United and Chicago Fire.

◀ *Defoe celebrates with Gareth Bale, after scoring for Spurs in a Champions League qualifying game in 2010.*

From the kick off, Tottenham put Wigan under pressure. They dominated possession and had shot after shot on the Wigan goal. Despite this, they were only 1–0 up at half time. But six minutes into the second half, Defoe scored his first goal of the afternoon. It was a trademark Defoe goal; he sprinted into the penalty box at just the right time to latch onto an Aaron Lennon cross. Defoe got in front of his **marker** and thumped the ball past the Wigan goalkeeper.

Tottenham Hotspur vs Wigan Athletic

On 22 November 2009, Tottenham Hotspur played host to
Wigan Athletic at White Hart Lane. As usual the Tottenham
players had their pre-match meal together. Defoe was relaxed;
he was having a great season. He was the highest scorer in the
Premier League, and was enjoying every minute of playing in
front of the Tottenham fans. His confidence was very high and
it seemed as if things
couldn't get any better
– then they did.

◀ *Defoe in his
Tottenham strip
in 2009.*

HIGH FIVE

Defoe moved to Tottenham for the first time in 2004, but moved to Portsmouth four years later. In 2009, Defoe was playing for Tottenham Hotspur again. He helped Tottenham to finish fourth in the Premier League in the 2009/2010 season. This meant the team qualified for the **UEFA** Champions League for the first time since 1961. Defoe was the club's leading goal scorer, with 24 goals. Without his goals, it is unlikely Tottenham would have qualified. One game in the 2009/10 season will ensure Defoe's name is remembered at the club for years to come.

▼ *Defoe playing for Portsmouth during a UEFA Cup match against Wolfsburg.*

RECORD BREAKERS

At 17, Jermain Defoe was on the verge of breaking into West Ham's first team. He had everything required to be a top-class striker in the Premier League; lightning speed, precision finishing and a unique instinct to be in the right place at the right time.

On loan at AFC Bournemouth

Harry Redknapp could see all of this in training every day. But he knew that Defoe needed to toughen up before he stepped up to the first team. With this in mind, he sent Defoe on **loan** to AFC Bournemouth. Here, he would get match practice against hardened professionals every week.

From the moment he arrived at Bournemouth, Defoe loved the atmosphere at the club. He scored on his **debut** and went on to set a new league scoring record by netting 10 goals in 10 successive games. His achievement meant that for the first time Defoe was creating headlines in the national newspapers.

Premier League debut

When Defoe returned to West Ham from his record-breaking loan spell, he was stronger, sharper and more experienced. Harry Redknapp decided that Defoe was now ready for football in the Premier League. He gave Defoe his debut at the start of the 2001/2002 season. For the next two years he was West Ham United's top scorer and became a regular in the England Under-21 team. Defoe finally left West Ham in 2004.

▶ *Defoe is tackled during an AFC Bournemouth vs Northampton Town match. Bournemouth won 3–0.*

The best coaches in England worked at Lilleshall. Their expertise, combined with Jermain's constant practice on the training ground, improved his all round game. When he arrived back at Charlton two years later he had transformed himself into a top-class player. Everyone watching him at Charlton knew that within a very short space of time he would be lining out for their first team.

West Ham United

Unfortunately for Charlton, West Ham United also had their eye on Defoe and they offered him a professional contract. Aged just 16, it was to prove the best move of Defoe's career. At the time, West Ham were managed by Harry Redknapp who recognised Defoe's talent. Redknapp encouraged Defoe to develop his physical strength in the gym and allowed him to train with the first team players. Within 18 months of signing for West Ham, Defoe scored his debut goal against Walsall in a League Cup game.

▲ *West Ham's Jermain Defoe drifts past the Chelsea goalkeeper during a FA Cup replay at Upton Park.*

Charlton Athletic

Defoe's goal-scoring instinct attracted the local **professional** clubs. He joined Charlton Athletic, and soon after he was offered a place at Lilleshall, the Football Association's (FA's) school for **elite** young players. This was the turning point in Defoe's footballing life. Every year, the FA selected 16 of the best young players in the country and gave them full-time **coaching**. At 14 years of age, Defoe was eating, training and living like a full-time athlete.

▲ *A football pitch at Lilleshall National Sports Centre. The centre's facilities are the best in the country.*

EASTENDER

Jermain Defoe was born in Beckton, East London on the 7 October, 1982. His mum and dad were originally from the Caribbean islands of St Lucia and Dominica. He grew up in a **council house** that he shared with his mother, Sandra and younger sister, Chonte. Defoe was raised in a close, loving family, but the area he lived in was poor. He witnessed drug dealing, joy-riding and violence throughout his youth.

Playing with passion

From an early age Defoe had a passion for football. He spent his free time playing matches on the streets and in the parks with his friends. He even went to school an hour early to have a kick around in the playground. Football was the only thing that mattered to him.

Defoe was a small boy, but even so he could control and **dribble** the ball better than most kids. Some are good at dribbling but Defoe had something extra – an incredible ability to score goals. It was this talent that made him stand out from the crowd.

School football team

When Defoe went to St Bonaventure's secondary school, he quickly made his way on to the school football team. With Defoe on board, St Bons eased their way into the Essex Schools Cup Final. To the amazement of everyone at the game, he scored six goals before half time. What made it even more impressive was the fact that he was the youngest player on the pitch.

▶ *England's Jermain Defoe during an international schoolboy match against Brazil in 1998.*

4:22 pm

England start the game with lots of energy, and they attack the Slovenia defence. Then James Milner receives the ball on the right-hand touchline. He looks up and plays a perfectly flighted ball into the **penalty box**. Defoe sprints in front of the Slovenia defender and volleys the ball into the net. GOAL! Defoe runs towards the corner flag to celebrate, his team-mates jump all over him. The England fans in the stadium cheer wildly. At last, England are playing well.

▲ *Defoe celebrates scoring in the South Africa 2010 World Cup Finals.*

5:50 pm – full time

The game has ended and the scoreboard reads: England 1 – Slovenia 0. On the sideline, Fabio Capello, the England manager, looks relieved. As Defoe walks off the pitch every one of his team-mates congratulates him. It doesn't get much better than this. He's playing at the World Cup and has just booked England's place in the last 16. ***But how did he get there?***

LONDON BOY – ENGLAND HERO

**England vs Slovenia – 23 June 2010,
Nelson Mandela Bay Stadium, South Africa.**

3:10 pm
Photographers and TV crews gather round the England team
bus as it pulls into the Nelson Mandela Bay Stadium. The door
opens and the England players walk swiftly to the dressing room.
Jermain Defoe strides confidently past the cameras. This afternoon
England are playing Slovenia in the final group game of the
2010 World Cup. They have to win if they are to progress to the
knockout stages.

3:25 pm – 35 minutes before kickoff
Fourteen million people are ready to watch the game live on TV.
Although the England team is packed with world-class players,
it performed poorly in the first two matches against the USA and
Algeria. Now the players must put in a top-class performance.

3:55 pm
Five minutes to kick off. The England team huddle together for
the final words of encouragement from captain Steven Gerrard.
Defoe listens to the chanting of the England fans and can feel the
buzz of the vuvuzelas sending vibrations through the stadium. His
adrenalin is starting to kick in. This is it!

Jermain Defoe
Contents

Acknowledgements:

Ben Angel/Action Plus/Topfoto: XIV. Matthew Ashton/Empics/PAI: XVIII. Chris Barry/Action Plus/Topfoto: VIII. CSM /Landov LANDOV/ Press Association Images: 15. Adam Davy/ Empics/PAI: XII. Paul Ellis/AFP/Getty Images: 18. Nigel French/EMPICS/PAI: XIII. Getty Images: XX. Laurence Griffiths/Getty Images: V. Mitchell Gunn/Action Plus/Topfoto: 13. Robert Hallam/Rex Features: VII. Richard Heathcote - The FA/The FA via Getty Images): 23. Andy Hooper/Daily Mail/Rex Features: IX. Tobias Kuberski /Action Plus: 20. Tony Marshall/ PAI: 7. Jamie McDonald/Getty Images: 9. Jeff Mitchell /Getty Images: 21. Peter Norton/ Allsport/Getty Images: XI. PA/PAI: 11. Nick Potts/PAI: back cover, 5. Professional Sport/ Topfoto: front cover. Rex Features: XVII. Jurie Senekal/Getty Images: XXI. Sipa Press/Rex Features: XXII. Mark Thompson/Getty Images: XXIII. Neil Tingle/Action Plus/Topfoto: 16, 19.

Every attempt has been made to clear copyright. Should there be any inadvertent omission please apply to the publisher for rectification.

Note: At the time of going to press, the statistics in this book were up to date. However, due to the nature of sport, it is possible that some of these may now be out of date.

W EDGE
FRANKLIN WATTS
LONDON·SYDNEY

Jermain Defoe is one of England's best strikers – he's a goal-scoring machine! Read all about his club and international football career inside – then flip over to find out more about Wayne Rooney.

RORY CALLAN

JERMAIN DEFOE

FOOTBALL ALL-STARS